A Book About Wolves
AMAZING EARTH: Wild Animal Facts
Written and designed by Dawon Seashore

COPYRIGHT © 2023 by Dawon Seashore

All rights reserved.
No part of this publication may be reproduced, stored in a retrieval system, stored in a database and / or published in any form or by any means, electronic, mechanical, photocopying, recording or otherwise, without the prior written permission of the publisher, except in the case of quotations embodied in critical reviews and certain other noncommercial uses permitted by copyright law.

Information contained within this book is for entertainment and educational purposes only. Although the author and publisher have made every effort to ensure that the information in the book was correct at press time, the author and publisher do not assume and hereby disclaim any liability to any party for loss, damage, or disruption caused by errors or omissions, whether such errors or omissions result from negligence, accident, or any other cause.

Dear reader,

We are happy to present to you A Book About Wolves. This book is part of our Wild Animal Facts series where we take a look at some amazing facts about Earth's many fascinating animals.

The book was created for all youngsters out there, and any curious adult, who love to learn more about their favorite creatures.

We sincerely hope you enjoy and have fun reading. After, you can find out if you learned something new in a fun quiz at the end of the book. There are lots of beautiful photos as well!

Be sure to leave a review to let us know how you liked the book. It helps a lot to improve and expand on future publications.

Sincerely yours,

Wild Animal facts Team

TABLE OF CONTENT

What are they?	7
Types of Wolf	11
How big are they?	12
What do they look like?	15
Where do they live?	18
What do they eat?	19
Wolf Pack	20
Communication	22
Behavior	24
Daily Life	26
Family Life	29
Interesting Facts	32
Lifespan	35
Future of Wolves	36
Conservation	37
Quiz Time!	38
Glossary	41

WOLF is a common name for many different types of wolves found in the wild. When we think 'wolf', the **gray wolf** (*Canis lupus*) usually comes to mind.

The gray wolf (common wolf) is also known as the timber wolf in North America, and the white wolf in the Arctic.

Timber wolf

White wolf

WHAT ARE THEY?

First of all, wolves are mammals* which means they have fur and feed their young with milk.

They are large canids from Eurasia and North America.

Most canids have:
1. long snouts with a great sense of smell
2. upright ears for better hearing
3. sharp, pointed teeth for tearing flesh
4. long legs built for running
5. long, bushy tails

CANID - an animal that is a member of the **Canidae** family

Canids are mostly social animals, living together in family units or small groups.

Group of wolves

*if the words in green are a bit hard for you to understand, look up what they mean in the glossary at page 41-42

The wolf is the largest living species of the family Canidae, a group of dog-like animals that also includes domestic dogs, foxes, jackals, coyotes, and some other species.

Dog (Labrador)

Red fox

Jackal

Coyote

The largest canid, the gray wolf, is 6.6 feet (2 meters) long while the smallest canid, the fennec fox, is only 9.4 inches (24 centimeters) long!

fennec fox

gray wolf

WOLVES vs COYOTES

Despite similarities, a coyote has a narrower snout, tall pointed ears, and is smaller compared to a wolf.

Wolf

Coyote

Even so, wolves are closely related to the coyote and golden jackal and can make babies with them.

Coywolf

Did you know?
The young of two animals that are of different species are called **hybrids**.

TYPES OF WOLF

Even though there are 30 known wolf types, many of them are simply subspecies of the gray wolf.

Some of these subspecies include the Eurasian wolf, Arctic wolf, Tundra wolf, and Steppe wolf.

Red wolves are a North American type of wolf not found anywhere else in the world. They live only in a small coastal area of North Carolina (NC), USA!

UNITED STATES OF AMERICA

Red wolves are critically endangered! There are less than a 150 of them left.

Red wolf

HOW BIG ARE THEY?

Adult wolves are 41–63 in (105–160 cm) long and 31–33 in (80–85 cm) tall at the shoulders. Their tail adds another 11–20 in (29–50 cm) to their length.

AVERAGE WOLF WEIGHT
European wolves: 85 lb (38.5 kg)
North American wolves: 79 lb (36 kg)
Indian and Arabian wolves: 55 lb (25 kg)

Females usually weigh 5–10 lb (2.3–4.5 kg) less than males.

European wolf

Indian wolf

Did you know?

The LARGEST subspecies of wolf in the world is the Northwestern wolf (also known as the **Mackenzie Valley wolf**, or Canadian timber wolf). An average male weighs up to 137 pounds (62 kilograms)! They are mostly found in Canada and Alaska.

WHAT DO THEY LOOK LIKE?

The wolf has very dense and fluffy winter fur, with a short undercoat and long, rough guard hairs. Most of the undercoat is shed in spring and grows back in autumn.

Its fur is usually made up of white, brown, gray, and black parts.

In the arctic, its fur may be all white.

Large and heavy head

It has four toes with claws in an oval shape.

Wolves have long, round ears.

They have a long snout full of sharp teeth.

A wolf's eye color is usually amber to pale yellow, or rarely green.

Did you know?

Blue, or dark brown/black eye color is extremely rare in wolves!

4 canines

Wolves have 42 teeth. The so-called canines are the largest and can grow up to 2.5 in (6.4 cm) long! They can be found in all canids, and there are usually 4 of them – two on the upper jaw and two on the lower one.

These teeth are used to crush bones and hold prey!

Wolf holding a chicken

WHERE DO THEY LIVE?

Wolves live in forests, wetlands, grasslands (including Arctic tundra), pastures, deserts, and rocky peaks on mountains.

These days, they live in many parts of the Northern Hemisphere. Different wolf subspecies are found in Eurasia as well as some parts of the Arabian Peninsula.

The largest wolf populations can be found in Canada, then Alaska and Russia.

NORTHERN HEMISPHERE = the half of Earth north of the Equator

Alaska
Canada
Russia
EURASIA
Arabian Peninsula
EQUATOR
SOUTHERN HEMISPHERE

WHAT DO THEY EAT?

Wolves are carnivores — they mostly eat other animals. They are also apex predators, which means they are on top of the food chain.

They hunt moose, deer, elk, and boar, or sheep and goats when available.

A group of deer

Beavers, rabbits, rodents, and birds will do if they can't find larger animals.

Wolves are NOT picky eaters! They also eat fish, apples, melons, and berries.

WOLF PACK

There are so-called "lone wolves" but most of them live in groups called packs. Typically, lone wolves are only alone before they join a pack or form their own!

A pack usually is made up of a mating pair followed by their young.

The average pack size in North America and Asia is 8 wolves, while in Europe 5-6 wolves. This includes two adults – male and female, juveniles, and cubs.

Young wolves stay in the pack for the first 10-54 months of their life. Later, they leave to find or form their own pack.

Did you know?

There is **NOT** really an "**alpha**" in a wolf pack! The leaders of a pack are simply the parents – one male and one female. These two are **dominant** over the other wolves in the pack. Only they are allowed to produce young wolves.

COMMUNICATION

The wolves' communication skills are very important for the pack's survival! Wolves communicate mostly using vocalizations, body language, and scent.

Vocalizations include howls, growls and barks, whimpers and whines, yelps and snarls.

Urination is one of the most important forms of scent communication among wolves. It is a more effective way to mark their territory than leaving scratch marks or howling!

Wolves howl to gather the pack before and after hunts, to warn of danger, to locate each other during a storm, and to communicate across great distances.

A wolf's howl can be heard as far as 10 miles (16 km) away in an open area!

BEHAVIOR

Wolves are territorial – they claim large areas as their own to secure a supply of prey. While traveling in search of prey, wolves cover roughly 16 miles/day (25 km/day)!

Once they catch prey, wolves eat hastily. The pack's leaders eat FIRST and secure food for their pups. After, the rest of the pack members eat.

Wolves typically overpower other canids in areas where they both live.

Wolves kill coyotes, red foxes and Arctic foxes in fights over food.

DAILY LIFE

Wolves are *nocturnal* hunters.

During the winter, a PACK starts hunting in twilight and continue all night.

During the summer, wolves tend to hunt ALONE and *ambush* their prey.

Each day, a wolf walks for about 8 hours, sometimes covering 30 miles per day!

Wolves living in packs walk for two basic reasons:
1. to capture food
2. to defend territory

Wolves searching for prey

Fight between wolves

FAMILY LIFE

Wolves mate once a year, usually in late winter (February to March). They usually stay with their partner for life.

Dens are usually built for pups during the summer period.

When building dens, females make use of natural shelters like cracks in rocks and holes covered by vegetation.

Usually, 4-6 wolves are born into a litter. Sometimes, this number can go up to 14!

Pups are born blind and deaf, covered in soft grayish-brown fur. They weigh only 0.66 - 1.1 lb (300-500 g) at birth.

Did you know?

Wolf pups grow fast during their first four months of life. During this period, a pup's weight can increase nearly 30 times!

Pups first leave the den after three weeks.

This is when wolf pups begin play-fighting with each other, while actual fights for domination usually begin at five to eight weeks of age.

By autumn, the pups are mature enough to follow the adults on hunts for large prey.

INTERESTING FACTS

1

Wolves have excellent smell and hearing. A wolf's sense of smell is 100 times stronger than a human's, and they can hear up to 6 miles (9.7 km) away!

2

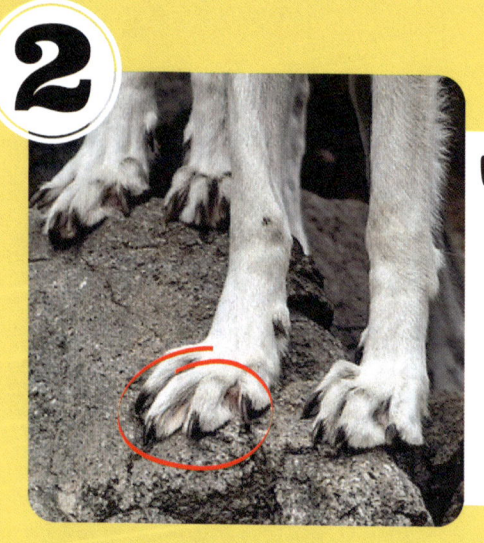

Wolves have WEBBED paws, or thin layers of skin between their toes. These "webs" allow wolves to swim distances of up to 8 miles (13 kilometers)!

Webbed wolves' paws

3

Many nocturnal and deep-sea animals have a special reflective layer in their eyes. This layer is called the <u>tapetum lucidum</u>, or 'bright tapestry'.

Cat's eye glowing in the dark

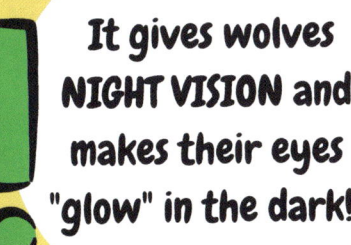

It gives wolves NIGHT VISION and makes their eyes "glow" in the dark!

4

Although wolves can see in the dark, humans have better eyesight when it comes to seeing color and distance.

Human eye

33

5

Wolves were first domesticated in northern Eurasia 14,000 – 29,000 years ago which resulted in dogs we know and love today! There are well over 300 breeds of dogs in the world, and they all come from wolves.

6

Siberian huski

German shepherd

Alaskan malamut

+ Wolf

+ Wolf

Wolfdog

Siberian huskies, German shepherds, and Alaskan malamutes can mate with wolves making a wolfdog.

LIFESPAN

Territorial fights are one of the main causes of wolf deaths. Research shows that in some cases more than half of wolf deaths are caused by other wolves!

Wolves can live up to 13 years **in the wild**.

In reality, this number is closer to 6-8 because of territory fights, starvation, and hunts by humans.

They can live up to 16 years **in captivity** – shelters, zoos, and alike.

FUTURE OF WOLVES

Wolves were once widespread but today there are only 200,000–250,000 of them left in the wild.

As a whole, they are considered of least concern but looking at individual types or populations of wolves, many of them are near extinction!

The wolf is now completely extinct in Ireland, the United Kingdom, and Japan.

In modern times, the wolf lives mostly in wilderness and remote areas.

CONSERVATION

In the US, wolves are protected under federal law. They are considered an endangered species since many types, like the red wolf, are nearly extinct.

In Canada, there are about 50,000-60,000 wolves left in the wild. This makes Canada an important sanctuary for wolves! Wolf hunts in Canada are regulated by law.

Europe, excluding Russia, Belarus and Ukraine, has 17,000 wolves in more than 28 countries. In many countries of the European Union, the wolf is strictly protected by law.

The wolf is also protected by law in some other countries like Israel, Oman, and India.

37

QUIZ TIME!

1. Which animal family do wolves belong to?
   a) Ursidae
   b) Ailuridae
   c) Felidae
   d) Canidae

2. Where is the largest population of wolves?
   a) in the USA
   b) in Mexico
   c) in Canada
   d) in Israel

3. What is a group of wolves called?
   a) a herd
   b) a pack
   c) a litter
   d) a pride

4. What eye color do wolves typically have?
   a) yellow
   b) green
   c) blue
   d) brown/black

5. What are wolves based on their diet?
   a) herbivores
   b) carnivores
   c) omnivores
   d) hypercarnivores

6. How many wolves are usually in a pack?
   a) only 2
   b) 1-4
   c) 5-8
   d) more than 10

7. When do wolves usually hunt?
   a) during the day
   b) at night
   c) during storms
   d) only during summer

8. Which animals come from domesticated wolves?
   a) cats
   b) coyotes
   c) foxes
   d) dogs

9. In which country are wolves NOT extinct?
   a) Israel
   b) Ireland
   c) Japan
   d) United Kingdom

Bonus question: ?

10. Who is the leader of a wolf group?
    a) the male alpha
    b) the female alpha
    c) the mating pair
    d) there is no leader

Did you finish the quiz? Well done!

Don't worry if you didn't know the answer to all of the questions at first.

You can go back and read through the book again to find the missing answers.

Hopefully you had fun reading and learned some new amazing facts about your favourite animal.

P.S.
Just in case you didn't manage to find all the answers in the end, we put them here for you to look up.
ANSWERS: 1.d), 2.c), 3.b), 4.a), 5.b), 6.c), 7.b), 8.d), 9.a), 10.c)

GLOSSARY

ambush: to make a surprise attack from a hidden place

apex predators: animals that are at the very top of the food chain. This means they hunt other animals, but are mostly not hunted themselves.

canid: member of the Canidae animal family

canines: long, pointed and sharp teeth in many mammals

carnivore: animal that mainly eats meat

den: the resting place of wolves, lions, and other large wild animals

domesticate (animals): raise animals to live close to humans as pets or working animals

dominant: having power, storength, or control over another

endangered: in danger of becoming extinct

extinct: no longer existing

guard hairs: the outer layer of the coat of some animals

hybrid: the young of two animals of different species

in captivity: animals that are held by humans and prevented from escaping, like in a shelter or zoo

in the wild: animals living free in nature

least concern (animal): type of animal there's still plenty of in the wild

litter: a group of young animals born to the same mother at the same time

mammals: animals with fur that feed their young with milk

mate: to make babies together

mating pair: a male and female of the same animal that make babies together

nocturnal: active mostly at night

pack: a group of wolves living and hunting together

population (of an animal): total number of an animal species living in an area

prey: an animal that is hunted or caught for food, usually by another animal

pup: the young of foxes, wolves, and some other animals

reflective: turns away light instead of absorbing it

sanctuary: land protected as a shelter for wild animals

social: living in groups or communities instead of alone

species (of animals): a group of animals that can come together to make babies with each other, but not with animals of other groups (species)

subspecies: a smaller group of animals within a species different from the other members

territorial: defensive over one's territory

territory (of animals): an area marked and defended by a type of animal

undercoat: fine fur under the outer (guard) layer of an animal's coat that keeps it warm

vocalization: a sound made with the voice

wolfdog: hybrid of a wolf and a dog

Congratulations!

You have come to the end of this book.

Thank you for reading this far. Here is an extra photo just for you!

Leave us a *review* on Amazon if you liked the book! ❤️

Printed in Great Britain
by Amazon